IN THEIR HANDS

a true story of the trusting

by

JoAnn D. Carol

A Hearthstone Book

Carlton Press, Inc. New York, N.Y.

Cover and sketch facing page 9 by ALEX

Manufactured in the United States of America
ISBN 0-8062-4350-3

CONTENTS

PREFACE

Recognizing that honest mistakes are made in the medical field as well as in any other profession in our society, this exposure reflects not upon those who would make honest mistakes, but, rather upon those who try to cover up the error, compounding the original innocent episode. Two wrongs never will make a right!

When a mistake causes a death, it is one of great magnitude. However, in the case in question, if there had been admissions of the error immediately, this life may have been saved and those responsible would look less like a group of incompetents.

This is a true story, the writer having kept a daily log throughout the entire happening. The medical facts contained in the story are substantiated by actual excerpts from the medical records as designated by block outline throughout.

NOTE THIS!

The place: A hospital in the northeast.

The year: 1984. The names have been changed for obvious reasons.

With the hope that this needless death may not have been in vain, the writer has a strong, compelling need to alert anyone contemplating surgery to make very sure, first of all, that the surgery is necessary. Secondly, and just as importantly, to have *A SECOND LOOK* at the pathologist report where biopsies are involved. Thirdly, ask questions even though the doctor either becomes aggravated because you ask, or tries to avoid answering.

The injustices experienced by this trusting victim and his family were so very unnecessary. If the doctors involved had dared to tell the truth from the beginning and had spent their time trying to save the patient instead of trying so hard to cover up, Joe just might have lived.

IN THEIR HANDS

ALEX

December 1983

The year 1983 ended with Joe's dad's funeral. His dad was our charge for nearly twenty years, all of the time lamenting that life had dealt him a hard blow when we lost Joe's mother. Now Joe and I could finally go to Florida for the winter months and not worry if his dad needed us.

It wasn't going to be that simple. While his dad was being prepared for the viewing, we learned that I had a lung tumor, the same diagnosis as Dad's. This was revealed while x-raying for a broken rib sustained while trimming the Christmas tree.

Dr. Small had called both Joe and me into his office, first telling of finding a tumor—then again to tell of finding not one, but three tumors!

January and February 1984

On January 3rd, I went to a hospital in a nearby city to begin the search for any hidden tumors (this was "procedure" I was told). The search revealed no further tumors. So on January 10th, I had surgery to remove a portion of the broken sixth rib for biopsy. The test was benign, so all being negative I was permitted to go home for the weekend, to return Sunday at noon, January 15th.

It was on this day while I was in surgery that Joe, having a cold, was somehow talked into going to radiology for a chest X-ray. He needed some personal attention, too, as he awaited my return from the operating room. The report on this X-ray was:

> Jan. 10. 1984—"The lungs appear satisfactorily ventilated from apex to diaphragmatic level. Heart and aorta are *not* abnormal. Diaphragmatic and pleural ranges present no unusual features."

The chief surgeon and his associate explained and diagrammed for me that the next procedure for my problem was to operate on my lung—promising me another fifteen years of life. The procedure entailed cutting a pie-shaped piece from the lung, encompassing the affected portion. For this I gave consent.

During the surgery, however, the entire upper lobe of the right lung was removed. I was not told why this was done, although I was told there had been two tumors. One was the size of a dime; the other very small. The larger one was malignant, I was told by a doctor later. I never did hear about the small one. The biopsy reports of the tumors were not included in my hospital records.

Then began the long recuperation. Joe sat with me each day in the hospital and became acquainted with the hospital's chaplain, Bruce

Long. In general, the hospital stay was adequate, however, my room was at the end of the hall and I believe the nurses forgot there were patients there. Some days as many as four hours passed without a nurse checking on my roommate or me.

The stitches had been removed and I was recovered enough to come home on the 25th of January. Joe insisted he could take care of me, and he did. Our daughter helped me with my shower for the first week, then Joe took this over, too. He gave me moral support, allowed me to nap while he answered my phone calls; did the cooking and got up with me in the middle of the night when I'd cry with muscle spasms and discomfort around the incision area and pain in the chest in one particular spot. Because of the soreness of my breast and this sore spot, I was taking pain pills and wearing a transcutaneous electrical nerve stimulating device (TENS) unit at the same time.

On February 20th, Joe and I went to see Dr. Snow, the associate surgeon, for the third post-operative visit, but he could not explain the reason for the sore breast, nor could he explain the reason for the sore spot or what to do about either except to take pain pills. He denied the use of metal for any inside sutures.

Several months later, after consulting a pulmonary specialist, I was told that my incision was made too high. This affected the nerves and left scar tissue in the area of the breast that needs to drain, blocking drainage. This was more probably the reason for my intense discomfort, in his opinion.

Not to be overlooked is the all too surprising fact that chest X-rays made in another hospital revealed plainly two one-half inch long staples in the lining of the lung (which is known to be very sensitive) and multiple wire staples throughout. The two long staples are located in the exact area of the pain I experienced. There is no mention of these staples in my hospital records.

However, a specialist in the field of hematology and oncology gave me the good news that I did not need any special treatment. The malignancy was gone; I should return in six months to see him.

Even though Joe had recently had an upper GI series made with negative results, because of problems with indigestion, on February 22nd he had a stomach and duodenum X-ray with oral barium, (at the persistence of Dr. Small, our family doctor). The hospital report of this reads:

"No intrinsic organic disease of stomach. Duodenal physiology was satisfactory. All okay."

On February 28th I cooked dinner, and with the first bite Joe had a problem. This wasn't anything new, it happened frequently that the first mouthful of food would get stuck in the esophagus and wouldn't go down. Usually after a few minutes all would be okay. However, half an hour passed and he didn't get relief. I called our son-in-law who said he'd take Joe to the doctor's if I'd keep our young grandson. Dr. Small took an EKG, and by the time Joe moved about and regurgitated, he was fine. He wanted to see Joe in a week or so.

March 1984

Life got a bit more complicated at this point. I had been working to finish our income tax, we were still cleaning some treasures from yesteryear (from Joe's dad's house), working on the sale of the house and occasionally babysitting our grandson.

We didn't need any more complications to our life, but now Joe, too, had a problem needing attention. On March 5th, Joe went to see Dr. Small who *insisted* on sending him to the hospital for a stomach search even though the X-ray had shown nothing unusual. We knew what Joe's problem *had been*—a hiatal hernia—but he finally agreed to go to the hospital for this test.

On March 6th at 9 a.m. an endoscopy was performed. The report reads:

> "The esophagus was examined in its entirety. G.E. junction was visualized. In the distal area of the esophagus, a modular, ulcerative infiltrate was noted. Two biopsies were obtained, bleed freely. Stomach and duodenum were negative. Impression: Ulcerative esophagitis with hiatal hernia. Will await biopsy report to rule out carcinoma."
> By Dr. Bow

The March 6th biopsy report reads as follows:

> "Clinical diagnosis: Esophagitis
> Tissue submitted: Biopsy of esophagus
> Microscopic exam: Multiple sections through the esophageal biopsy demonstrates an occasional fragment of normal esophagus. The bulk of this tissue consists of hyperplastic esophageal mucosa with keratin formation and hyperchromatic nuclei. In one area this change becomes more malignant and the cells invade through the basement membrane."
> Pathological diagnosis: "Squamous cell carcinoma of esophagus Class A."
> Signed by Dr. Falco M.D., 3/7/84

On Wednesday, March 7th, at noon, there was an urgent call from Dr. Small. Both of us were expected at the doctor's office immediately. I was, at this point, getting used to bad news, so upon arrival I asked, "Don't tell me you have bad news again for us?"

His answer, "Yes, I do—Joe has a malignant tumor in his esophagus—they are waiting for you at the hospital."

We had no reason to question the report of the pathologist. After all, Joe's father and mother both died of cancer, also several aunts and uncles. We thought it quite logical and entirely possible for Joe, too, to have cancer.

So with much apprehension about the unknown, we rushed home to get ready to go to the hospital. Two income tax customers who had appointments with me were there. I began to explain to each that I'd be in touch with them for a future appointment, when the door bell rang and there stood a couple of our antique dealer friends from mid-Pennsylvania whom we had invited for a few days' visit. It was the first time they had been to our place, but obviously there would be no visiting today since the doctor who did the endoscopy, Dr. Bow, was waiting for Joe.

As Joe changed, I made our apologies and put his robe and slippers in a small suitcase. As it turned out, we needn't have hurried; Dr. Bow had already left the hospital. I really feel that Dr. Small uses this hurry tactic—"They're waiting for you"—as a means of assuring that you'll go to the hospital without having time to change your mind or otherwise refuse.

So began the thirty-four-day stay in the hospital, beginning with an attempt to place a cardiovascular catheter (CVC) under the right collar bone; six large needle marks denoting six tries by a girl intern, while the chaplain held his hand. Dr. Ben, a male intern, was called in to finally do the job on the left side. Joe said it really hurt each time, but he cooperated until the successful try.

By now the chaplain and Joe had developed quite a rapport. Both were very tall and bearded men and they called themselves "Brothers of the Beard." Never having had a brother and feeling the need for special friendship, Joe put a lot of hope and faith in this man.

The Intravenous Solution (IV) was made up specifically for Joe, we were told. According to our informant, it cost $100 per bottle and was composed of minerals, vitamins and nutrients to prepare Joe's body for the radiation treatments, planned to be given immediately at a nearby hospital by Dr. Orr, a radiologist. Joe had taken these massive doses of carbohydrates only a day or so when his blood sugar rose drastically, requiring insulin shots with testing of urine every six hours. Up to now he had not been sick nor had he been losing weight. This treatment seemed so unnecessary.

For several years, Joe had followed the natural way to good health, studying vitamins and minerals and taking daily average amounts, keeping in shape.

Reports of Joe's X-rays of 3/8/84 are:

> X-ray, 3/8/84 — Complete lungs:
> "Heart not enlarged. No evidence of active inflammatory or congestive disease."
>
> X-ray, 3/8/84 — Abdomen:
> "X-ray ok."
>
> 3/8/84 Dr. Orr typewritten report:
> "The endoscopy report *was not available* to me when I saw the patient."
>
> Oral report:
> "Patient has squamous cell cacinoma of the esophagus. Best handled by preoperative radiation therapy followed by resection. Without chemotherapy dosage of radiation of 4500 rads can be delivered in a more rapid course of 3½ weeks. Followed by at least 1 month wait for tumor regression before surgery is attempted."

March 13th was a typical wintery day with snow already on the ground followed by sleet. I called Joe this day before and after his second trip for radiation. This was the first day I didn't see him, and although I called, it wasn't the same. He missed me and told everyone that he was "climbing the walls" without me. He called for the chaplain.

Following Joe's first radiation treatment he had indigestion so bad, then began to become nauseous and depressed. He was getting Mylanta every two hours. At my suggestion they began giving him small meals five times a day, trying to make him more comfortable. This helped somewhat.

This same day, I was taken to the Operating Room (OR) by the anesthetist, who gave me the first of five planned nerve blocks, trying to alleviate my pain by changing the course of nerve action. This first block had favorable effects, the second and third had little or no effect, so the plan was discontinued.

March 13 was a typical wintery day with snow already on the ground followed by sleet. I called Joe this day before and after his second trip for radiation. This was the first day I didn't see him, and although I called, it wasn't the same. He missed me and told everyone that he was "climbing the walls" without me. He called for the chaplain.

The plan was to have Joe receive a series of radiation treatments followed by surgery to remove a section of the distal portion of the esophagus. *We were told we were getting the benefit of a team of doctors' opinions* as was the policy of this hospital in severe cases. This gave us the confidence of having many opinions, and so our trust was given to these doctors.

March 14th—Joe had his third radiation treatment followed by horrible indigestion. All the while Joe tolerated severe indigestion Dr. Bow kept telling him how very optimistic he was that they could get all the affected part of the esophagus by surgery or radiation, or both.

The next day Joe was feeling a little better—not so much indigestion. Dr. Bow had prescribed something for the nausea, also a large pill for antacid.

By March 22, 1984, Joe was still suffering from indigestion—his stomach was badly swollen and since he didn't want T.V., they moved him to room #221, away from a roommate who wanted T.V. on till late at night. The nurses were very good to him; he was pathetically cooperative. On a typical day he took his nap and as I slept on a chair at the foot of his bed, a small nurse tiptoed quietly in and covered me with a white hospital blanket. I was so tired and *not* yet recovered from my recent surgery—just couldn't go all day.

I sat with him nearly all afternoon and evening during this first hospitalization. Sometimes I'd want so badly to be home where I could rest much better and I'd ask Joe if he wanted me to stay till evening—he'd usually answer, "It's up to you." Sometimes I *would* go home early, but knew he'd rather I'd stay. He listened to the news on his radio and he did some reading but found it hard to concentrate.

> X-ray March 26th—from records:
>
> "Complete lungs—heart *not* enlarged. The lungs are free from active inflammatory and congestive disease. There is some slight increased density in the left apex which may be artifactual. Old films were not available for comparison since they have been signed out to radiation therapy and are not available for review at this time. When chest film is compared with old report it appears to be similar."

On March 26th I came down with a virus with a sore throat. I went quickly to see Dr. Small who gave me some medication. I didn't go to the hospital for a couple of days but joined Joe by phone in his countdown of radiation treatments, five more to go. Joe was getting a kick out of the young nurses trying to find a hospital gown large enough for him. He wore his pajamas during the day, but liked the gown for sleeping and for getting the insulin shots in his shoulder. He said they had no gowns for "men"; Joe was a big man! Upon entering the hospital he stood 6′1″ tall, weighed about 220 lbs. He had a large frame—the stature and looks of John Wayne (when he didn't have his beard) or a look-alike for Burl Ives when he *did* have a beard.

His hands were quite large, with tapered fingers, chubby, with a ring size too large to be measured on a regular ring-sizing scale. He had a 42″ waist, wore a size 44 coat, kept his weight down and his waistline trim.

April 1984

By April 2nd, Joe had had fifty-five bottles of the powerful IV, seventeen radiation treatments, an additional eight inches on his waistline, about twenty lbs. additional, was feeling worse, throwing up and in general wanting to come home.

> April 3, 1984 — Dr. Orr, M.D.:
>
> "Radiation therapy patient will complete 4500 rads to the esophagus tomorrow. I would recommend a 3 week rest period to allow for as much regression of the edema from treatment. This will make resection much more easy. *The ideal window for surgery after this dose is 3 to 6 weeks.* Please see my consultation of 3/8/84."

April 4, 1984—Excerpts from a letter from Dr. Orr, Radiologist to Dr. Bow.—

Today, Mr. Joe——completed his planned course of radiation therapy. Histopathologic examination reveals this to be a squamous cell carcinoma of the esophagus. *This was reportedly in the distal esophagus but despite multiple requests the endoscopy report has never been sent to me.* His upper G.I. series in late February was within normal limits and did not demonstrate any kind of obstructive phenomenon or lesion in the distal esophagus. *As a matter of fact the fluoroscopist made the statement in his report that there was no delay in the esophageal transit of oral barium.*

The patient has had a rather large dose of radiation in a moderately short period of time, and, for that reason I generally recommend as I did in my consult that the patient have a rest period before surgery. This allows for mucosal regeneration as well as a decrease in the radiation edema. The ideal window for surgery is 3–6 weeks post radiation *in order to also operate before radiation fibrosis begins in this area.*

Instead, this advice was not heeded. Joe was told to return to the hospital in 54 days. The actual surgery was performed two weeks later than was advisable to avoid radiation fibrosis.

April 4, 1984—This day finished his eighteenth radiation treatment followed the next day by another endoscopy. Dr. Bow says, "Tumor is still there," but the area was so bloody, surgery would not take place until four to six weeks.

April 5, 1984—Dr. Bow

"Endoscopy—patient was premedicated and esophagus was examined in its entirety. G.E. junction visualized and esophageal inflammation was noted secondary to radiation. *Tumor was still present.* The mucosa was friable."

"Impression: Esophagitis secondary to radiation and esophageal carcinoma."

April 5, 1984—Dr. Ben

> "Following endoscopy diapharatic airway partially obstructed. 32Fl nasal airway inserted three different times @ 44 min. monitor ROR. Hyperinfusing JB 0935 not as diapharitic. Skin not as clammy. Also suctioned for small amount-thick mucus."

April 10, 1984 — X-ray

> CT Scan normal, abdomen normal, heart normal, EKG was within normal limits.

April 10th, Joe was discharged with instructions to return for surgery June 4th. (54 days)

After thirty-four days of confinement, Joe was so glad to be home! He was very weak, somewhat nauseous, but all ready to plan the future—after the scheduled surgery. The very next day after he came home he had me call Florida to make reservations for the antiques shows there.

For the past eight years, Joe had helped me with buying and selling antiques. He drove our pickup truck, pulling our trailer to weekend trips of selling and to auctions to buy. He'd help put the merchandise out, be there to cover the stand in case of rain, and help to repack to come home. He loved meeting the other dealers, mostly couples like ourselves, and had a good social time talking with the customers. This activity gave us something to do with a common interest and gave me a little time away from the desk.

Gradually, Joe's appetite returned. He could eat spaghetti and sausage and other Italian recipes he loved, but by April 14th he had developed a cold. Dr. Bow had given him some cough syrup and said his cough was from the radiation. His cough wasn't considered at all serious by Joe, nor by either of his doctors, but I was concerned about it.

So we took up our lives where we had left off about a month ago, getting antiques ready to sell, having dinners at our favorite local restaurant, playing with or babysitting our only grandson, enjoying the get-togethers with our two daughters and their families, Joe taking me to the doctors for checkups, and going himself to the dentist with a problem tooth.

After three post-operative visits to Dr. Hackett's office and three nerve blocks, I was still suffering the same pain which followed my surgery in January. My daughter, Debra, decided to make an appointment with his assistant, Dr. Snow, since from past experience, he was easier to talk with than Dr. Hackett.

This she did for April 20th, but after we were ushered into the room, the nurse told us Dr. Hackett would be seeing us instead of Dr. Snow. Our big mistake was to stay, but we had traveled an hour to get there and my daughter had taken off work.

We had requested my chest X-rays taken March 22. Dr. Hackett said, "You requested to see your X-rays? What did you want them for? You can't read them anyway!" Needless to say we didn't get to see the X-rays. (These are described on February 20th, third paragraph.)

He then asked, "How is your husband?"

I answered, "He's really pretty good, but he's apprehensive about the coming surgery."

His snappy answer was, "Well, if you don't want me to operate on him, you can take him to another hospital." (He named a specific hospital.)

With this, he left the room, while we stood there in shock! When he returned, I told him Joe had asked me to find out if he knew yet just where he would be cut, down the middle or around from center to shoulder blade.

His answer was, "I don't know. I looked down with the endoscope but it was too bloody, so I really didn't take a good look." (This he did on April 5th.) I told him this was all I wanted to know. We left without satisfaction, but with confusion and hurt.

I had not expected Dr. Hackett's nasty attitude, and, to think a man this bad-natured was going to operate on Joe! I tried to talk to Joe about it, but he said he had made up his mind to go back to that same hospital, mostly because of the chaplain and the friendly care the nurses gave him during the thirty-four days he was there getting radiation. He figured the surgery would take only a few hours and then he'd be among friends for his recuperation. After all, *I* had come through surgery at the same place. The surgeon was the senior surgeon in this hospital.

On April 24th I was so upset! Joe was awaiting surgery and the surgeon was being so impossible! So Joe and I went to see Dr. Small. I related to him my episode with Dr. Hackett. I thought he was very understanding. He gave me some words of consolation, some medication and told me Dr. Hackett was due for a vacation. This was a help, but although he said he would not say anything to Dr. Hackett, it was obvious later that he did. His support for this man was unreal. Could it be that this hospital had sponsored Dr. Small, and he was obligated to be supportive to this hospital and to their main surgeon?

April 29th normally would have been a busy day for us. This is the opening day at the Grove where we would have been setting up for a weekend of selling antiques. But instead, Joe drove me to the hospital to see Dr. Yam the respiratory doctor, because I had coughed up some blood-streaked mucus. He looked into my bronchial tubes via bronchoscopy and found everything clear. Joe mowed the lawn this day for the first time this season but had an uneasy stomach all day and had to hire help to pick up sticks and in general clean up the backyard so he could mow with the riding mower.

May 1984

Saturday, May 5th, we drove to the Grove for a visit with dealer friends and to reserve space to sell after Joe's coming surgery. We really enjoyed the day; met more than a half dozen couples who wished us well.

Our days in early May were full of pricing antiques, refilling antique cases, grass cutting, planting a flower bed with azaleas and rhododendrons, dental appointments, both taking an afternoon nap, doing grocery shopping in a nearby community and eating out perhaps three or four times a week.

Although the doctor didn't ask to see Joe about his cough, he was still coughing from deep down, he kept taking naps off and on during the day. It seemed he needed the rest.

Still planning for his life after surgery, we sent for reservations at KOA camp to go to the World's Fair first, then over to Deland for the antique shows and to stay in Florida till April 1st, 1985.

On May 30th, Joe visited his Aunt Anna, an 89-year-old amputee with diabetes and a heart condition. On the way home from her place, we stopped at the local hospital to visit a friend, an ex-Mayor of a small town with approximately 5,500 inhabitants and Joe's hometown. I guess Joe realized what it means to have friends visit when you are sick or hospitalized.

The next day, Joe's barber came to the house and cut Joe's hair and trimmed his beard, getting ready for his pending hospital stay. He had packed his suitcase already. His last few days at home he became depressed. I could tell he was worried, but he maintained a positive attitude through it all. He kept telling everyone he didn't invite this cancer into his body—so he was going to get rid of it—and go on with the rest of his life. He told everyone who asked that he felt like a million bucks—no trouble swallowing nor with indigestion.

June 1984

Joe was sure that when he went back to the hospital, they would look down again with the endoscope and would find *no* tumor and would not operate.

Knowing it would again be necessary for another CVC (a painful ordeal as previously described in March), we asked Dr. Bow if this IV line could possibly be put in while Joe was anesthetized for the endoscopy. Alas—"procedure" dictated they would *not* look down prior to the surgery—but surgery would take place regardless, as per Dr. Bow.

Joe returned to the hospital June 4th, expecting surgery the following day. A couple of the doctors, including Dr. Bow, told Joe they didn't expect to see him back at the hospital for this surgery. (I can't figure exactly what was the reason for this expectation.) One of the nurses told me later she wanted so badly to tell Joe, "Don't have this done," but was fearful of losing her job if she did and was quoted.

Joe was given an EKG, chest X-ray and blood tests the first day and CAT Scan and barium X-ray of the stomach June 5th and 6th.

June 4, 1984—Results of Complete Lung study:

> Two projectional study compared with 3/26/84, the aortic arch is mildly dilated and sclerotic. The heart is average in size. Lungs are well ventilated with the exception of some coarsening of the left infrahilar bronchovascular markings constituting a change in appearance in the region.

June 5, 1984—CT of the Thorax

> Revealed a slight pleural thickening in the left lower lung zone.

Results of the barium X-ray of esophagus
June 6, 1984—(Day prior to surgery).

> At fluoroscopy the swallowing mechanism was satisfactory. There was no delay in the esophageal transit of oral barium. There was noted esophageal mucosal ring of schatski. Some gastro-esophageal reflex. The conventional films support the fluoroscopic examination. *No definite evidence of tumor.*

There really was no purpose in taking these tests; they were ignored! Procedure again! An endoscopy was not done.

On June 6th Dr. Hackett sent Dr. Snow along with Dr. Key and another intern, to talk with Joe and me about Joe's surgery to take place the next morning. Dr. Snow explained that Dr. Hackett had decided to cut the front of Joe, up from the naval and to the side, like two incisions. He told us of the risk involved, namely the possibility of leakage of the esophagus after the surgery, in which case it meant a few more days in the hospital—no real problem. This was the only risk he mentioned. Dr. Snow said the same as Dr. Small had said, that if *he* needed surgery he'd have Dr. Hackett. Was this to convince us of Dr. Hackett's credibility? He wanted me to sign for the surgery as well as Joe. I asked him if it was customary for the spouse to sign when the patient was capable. He answered, "No."

I asked, "Why now, then?"

He said, "Because Dr. Hackett isn't here to talk about this himself." I felt this was a lame excuse, but let it pass by.

In retrospect, I believe Dr. Hackett wanted to get out of doing this surgery, but wasn't man enough to politely decline. I believe he was apprehensive about this particular surgery, but could not admit it to his peers nor to the interns who followed him around like little children. He undoubtedly was trying to make me mad enough to get him "off the hook." If the patient had been my child, I would have immediately been looking for another surgeon, but since it was my husband, I had to respect his wishes; it was *his* body.

Getting Joe prepared for surgery, he first had to take some citrate of magnesia to get rid of the barium from yesterday's X-ray, followed by an enema. He wasn't in favor of any of this!

Joe knew I didn't want him to have surgery by this doctor, but he wanted to get the surgery behind him and "get on with the rest of his life." So our relationship this day before surgery was a bit strained. It would soon be time for me to leave, and I wondered if I should make one last try. But then I realized that if I had not been able to change his mind in the last six weeks, I wouldn't accomplish anything in our last hour except to upset us both. So I sat on the bed beside him, told him I loved him, and kissed him "Goodnight."

On June 7, 1984, Thursday, we arrived at the hospital around noon. Joe was still in surgery, as he had gone in at the earlier scheduled time. Carol, our oldest daughter, took me into town where we had some lunch and came back to the hospital about 3 p.m. My youngest daughter, Debra, was there with her husband, Lew. Joe had just been put in the recovery room after five hours and forty-five minutes of surgery.

Dr. Hackett met us and said Joe had had extensive surgery but was doing fine. He didn't indicate that there had been any problems. The chaplain came on the scene and got us all in to see Joe in the recovery room and then we waited to see him in the intensive care unit (ICU). Joe nodded, squeezed our hands, but could not talk because of the tube in his throat. The anesthetist came out from the operating room (OR) looking rather exhausted and said he was going to keep Joe on the respirator for the next twenty-four hours, just to make him more comfortable. He didn't act like the respirator was a necessary device—just a means of giving Joe less of a struggle in breathing. He, too, said everything was fine.

On June 7, 1984, Dr. Young describes the operation:

Those present:	Dr. Hackett, Key, Stone, Young, Conlin (extern third year)
Procedure:	Distal esophogectomy Esophagus gastrostomy Feeding tube Spleenectomy Thoracotomy-rib invertion (rib block)
Specimen:	Benign

June 7, 1984, Excerpts from the surgeon's report of the operation:

> As the short gastrics were ligated, a small laceration of the spleen was encountered and therefore the spleen was removed.
> No evidence of tumor was found during surgery.
> Frozen section of esophagus was negative.

This report mentions "the lung freed from adhesions"—but no mention was made of *how* this was done in regard to stitching, etc.

The chaplain had told Joe he would be there for him during surgery and after, however, we didn't see him for over a week directly after Joe's surgery. I wasn't aware he planned to be away from the hospital. He had promised me to be intermediary between Dr. Hackett and myself and had promised Joe he'd look after me, but when we needed him he wasn't there.

With ICU visiting hours being a half hour, 1 p.m., 5 p.m., and 8 p.m., we had to curtail our visiting to these hours. Worse yet, we had to depend on uncooperative ICU nurses to find out anything about Joe since he couldn't talk and there was never a doctor available. The chaplain could have been of help if he had made himself available as he had promised.

June 7, 1984—Clinical Diagnosis CA esophagus tissue submitted:

> 1. Spleen
> 2. Omentum
> 3. Rib cartilage
>
> 1. No evidence of gross tumor is seen.
> 2. No neoplastic lesions are seen.
> 3. No unusual gross lesions are noted.
>
> Pathological Diagnosis:
> 1. Spleen—no significant histopathologic features.
> 2. Omentum—No lesions.
> 3. Rib cartilage—No gross lesions Class A.

On the eighth day of June, I saw Joe at 1 p.m. and waited in the ICU waiting room to see him again at 5 p.m. He was awake, alert and asking for pain medication. He was still on the respirator and signalled to Debra and me he'd be on it for another twenty-four hours. It was very difficult to understand what he was trying to tell us (like charades). I did find out from the nurse that his blood pressure had been very low yesterday, 60/40, 80/65, but today it was up again, near normal. The tube down his throat bothered him. He also had a tube down his nose into his stomach. There were two IV's in the right arm, one was for blood plasma. He had two incisions, one from his navel up about eight inches (41 staples) and another around the right side of his chest (23 staples). There were also two drain tubes out his right side. I later noticed the tube directly into his intestine for feeding.

I surely wished we had studied and played the game of charades more often. Joe would gesture a message with his hands, fingers or facial expressions. Sometimes it was very difficult to understand exactly what he meant, so I found a clipboard and brought from home several unlined sheets of paper and a pen that would write upside down. This was a great help for our communication except that the doctors or nurses kept running off with the pen.

On June 9th, he wrote that he had a lung infection. However, a nurse said there was nothing on his chart to indicate infection, no elevation of temperature. He didn't want us to leave but kept dozing while we talked. He wanted so badly to get that tube out of his throat.

Sunday, June 10th—I saw Joe twice, 1 p.m. and 5 p.m. He was awake both times, and wrote on the pad to answer questions. I saved all the sheets of writing so I could ask him later what he meant—also to show his degree of alertness while one of the doctors recorded him as non-responsive. About 2 p.m. the nurse discovered he had a temperature—they gave him an antibiotic and Tylenol and had the X-ray machine in to see if the tubes were still in place.

Later that evening around 10 p.m. when I called ICU, the nurse said they were having trouble with the oxygen level. Joe's surgery was the 7th, Thursday, and by the 10th, Sunday, he was having trouble. Dr. Yam had the weekend off; I was told he'd be back Monday. He was the hospital's respiratory doctor; *the interns* would be looking after Joe in his absence.

June 11th—when my daughter Carol called the hospital between 9 and 10 a.m., she was told Joe's temperature was down from 103 degrees to 100 degrees and was told he seems okay.

Our granddaughter, Kim, came to visit Joe to say "Goodbye"; she would be leaving for camp in the morning. She kissed her Pop Pop

"Goodbye," just as the nurse was injecting valium again. As Kim left the room, it was evident Joe wanted to tell me something. I quickly got his glasses, pad and pen, and even though very groggy because of the valium, Joe tried desperately to write what he couldn't say. I picked his pen up for the third time and said, "Oh, honey, you're just too sleepy, can't you tell me this tomorrow?" He shook his head negatively and again tried to write. This time he managed to write four very short (three or four) letter words and dropped off to sleep. When I looked at the message I nearly cried—for, after all the trouble he had writing it, I could not understand it. I asked the nurse if she could read it—and while we looked at it together, I finally had a ray of light. I noticed a capital "K" and a small "m." After I decided this meant "Kim"—without the "i"—I read the next word where the first letter looked like a "9." Turned up to the right it was a "G," followed by "i" and "v." So he had left off the "e." The word was "Give." Now we have "Give Kim"—then the third word "fiv" another "e" left off. "Give Kim five dollars." Of course, the child was going to camp!

I saw Joe three times this day, 1–5–8 pm. He was more sedated than previously. I talked with Dr. Yam. He said Joe had fluid on the lung that was caused by surgery and then somehow it spread to the other lung. They had increased the pressure of the oxygen in the respirator, making Joe more uncomfortable, so they increased the sedation. Dr. Yam told me he had had this condition before with other patients and said he could handle it.

I shall never forget what happened Tuesday, June 12, about 1 p.m. Joe was in a cubical of the ICU that had windows across the top where on approaching the room one could see the patient in bed. As I approached the room, I could see Joe's face looked distorted. So I ran into his room and couldn't believe my eyes. Joe's right eye was completely swollen shut; on closer look I could see his upper torso was all swollen. He was completely sedated and unaware anything had gone wrong. I ran out of the room to find a nurse—intensive care indeed! Thinking she had been with her patient recently, I asked, "What's wrong?"

She knew I was really upset, but asked, "What do you mean?"

I answered, "Look at my husband, he's all swelled up!"

She then said this must have "just" happened and that she had called the doctor. I felt very sure she hadn't even noticed and that she couldn't have called the doctor yet. When I tried to find out what on earth could have happened, the nurse said, "I've never seen anything like

6/11/84

TOMORROW MORNING

IS IT

I HAVE 20 Yrs

IF

6/11/84 Mon eve.

9'YL Kn FiV Cdr

6/8

I Am going TO declAR
my SElf IN morning

s/5

Valium

I could use a big
drink of water +! A.
We sure blew that Valium

6/13/54

Can't I have

the lips

"Can't I have a sip of water?" →

water

Nurse said, "No water."
I reminded her of swabs to wet his mouth.
He nodded "yes" and nurse used swabs in his mouth.
Intensive care, indeed!

Nurse!

Cup

GLASSES

(ZIPPER?)

this before." She then proceeded to usher me out of the ICU telling me she'd let me know after the doctor looked at Joe. I waited in shock for a half hour!

Dr. Yam came to me after seeing Joe. He said the pressure of the oxygen on the respirator had burst a hole in the right lung, and the drain tube taking waste out of the chest cavity had become clogged. Consequently, the result was what hit me as I walked in the room. The air went under his skin and swelled up all excess tissue like eyelids and scrotum. He must have been very uncomfortable! Dr. Yam assured me this looked a lot worse than it really was. He said his heart and kidneys were okay and told me to "hang in there."

Joe looked about the same on June 13th. His eye was badly swollen, cheek swollen, and still heavily sedated with valium. The doctor tried cutting back (oxygen) on the respirator, but had to return to the previous setting.

Joe was still writing notes but was terribly groggy most of the time. He was getting high amounts of oxygen, and I was told his oxygen level was much better. They began giving Joe a diuretic. I guess they thought the swelling might be due in part to fluid rather than totally from the burst of air from the hole in the lung.

Late Thursday, Debbie and I talked with Dr. Ben, an intern Joe had grown fond of. He had been in this same hospital for a year and was awaiting his coming graduation, apparently working with any of the doctors. He told us the right lung was still collapsed following surgery. It had been adhered to the back or to another organ and Dr. Hackett cut through the pleura to free it, exposing that open part of the lung to the fatty tissue of his back. He said the lung was badly bruised. The PEEP (positive pressure) of the respirator was too much for the already damaged lung and blew a hole in it. They still said the lung would heal.

At bedside every day, sometimes twice a day, the portable lung was wheeled in and X-rays made.

> June 13, 1984: A P Projection reveals increase in the subcutaneous emphysema which is seen bilaterally and extending up into the neck. Other findings are reduced ventiliation in the left lower lung zone adjacent to the cardiac border. A similar finding seen on the right side.

June 13, 1984: Plan is to continue to decrease CO_2 until 50% or less and then gradually decrease PEEP.

June 14, 1984: 10:30 AM Dr. Ben goes on rounds. Apparently one chest tube not draining.

June 15, 1984: Infectious disease (extensive report) from Dr. Black, Infectious Disease Consultant.

On Friday, June 15, when I went in to see Joe at 1 p.m., he was restless. At one point he grabbed my hand to help pull himself up, almost to a sitting position, then settled to his side. He kept moving his legs and threw back the sheet as though to show me his testicles were swollen badly, as well as his upper body.

Dr. Snow made a point of seeing me this day in Joe's room. He had stopped the valium and started morphine to keep him still and quiet (he said). He also said Joe would be okay. Dr. Snow was the assistant surgeon working under Dr. Hackett. It was hard to tell which doctor was in charge of Joe's case, they kept changing.

Our son-in-law, Lew, enlarged a picture of Josh, our only grandson, and hung it from the ceiling. Joe opened his left eye and gave a half of a smile; he loved that little boy!

6/16/84—"Extensive subcutaneous emphysema bilaterally. Interstitial and alveolar disease—left lung zone. Some incomplete expansion seen on right side."

On June 16th my call to the hospital at 9:00 a.m. got the usual response from the nurse assigned to take care of Joe—"a day at a time." Many times I'd call, at the designated times, and would get a very "I don't know, I don't care" kind of answer. I called again between 1 and 2 p.m. and found they had made some X-rays, but hadn't read them yet. I did find out Joe was still on morphine. They wanted him to be very still so the PEEP could do its job.

I went to the hospital this day at 4:00 p.m. Joe was sound asleep. I needed to get some answers, so I asked for Dr. Ben. He generally was in the hospital after the others had left. He came and explained that Joe had developed pneumonia; both lungs were affected. He was on antibiotics and had a temperature. He acted like there was not much hope of reversing the problems.

I believe it was at this point I realized Joe wasn't going to make it. I was upset! Debbie heard what I heard but refused to believe it. Her Daddy couldn't die, he was so positive about living, he'd pull through!

> 6/16/84—"Operation—insertion of Swans-Ganz right sided heart catheter." (There was no permission given for this—didn't even say they were going to do this.) "Incision in left arm—catheter inserted about 25 cm. and procedure had to be aborted. Attempts from left side were fraught with multiple difficulties and, therefore, this was aborted. This was followed by cut down to clavicle—16 gauge catheter was put into subclavian vein. The Swans-Ganz catheter was then inserted and directed onward until it went through the right ventricular chamber and up into the pulmonary artery and out into the wedged segment. Appropriate pressure was obtained. Chest X-ray was obtained post-operatively."
> Dr. Key, D. O. Resident

Three tries to get one successful insertion of the catheter! It must have been torture for Joe.

A nurse's report one day stated, "Family here asking questions, the same questions over and over again." I wondered what she was afraid she'd tell.

We got the same old story from Dr. Snow on Sunday, June 17th. He said Joe's condition was the same—no better—no worse. His blood gases were 58 when they should have been 100. He told us there were two problems: 1. Double pneumonia which was being fought with antibiotics. 2. Adult Respiratory Distress Syndrome (RDS) which was being fought with the Positive Pressure Respirator (PEEP). He said Joe had a 50/50 chance of surviving. This, to me at that time, was just a way of pacifying the family.

Since the rule of ICU were visiting one-half hour every four hours, I tried to visit Joe at least two of the visiting periods. I had been staying all day in the ICU waiting room to see Joe three times but they had him so heavily sedated he didn't know I was there half the time—so I began going up, visiting, and coming home with the daughter who took me up.

When I didn't go to the hospital until 4:00 p.m., I always called ICU between 9 and 10 a.m. and sometimes again at 1 p.m. On the morning of the 18th I called the hospital about 9:05 a.m and Dr. Yam was looking in on Joe at the time. He said he'd talk with me at 1 p.m. Carol called at 1 p.m. and Dr. Yam said they had done a heart catherization and that his heart was fine. I did not see the need for this.

He explained how he planned to start a different respiratory method of high frequency ventilation that day. He also told us that Dr. Black, an infection specialist, had been called in on the case. Joe's temperature was normal, heart and kidney good, and Dr. Yam still had hopes of Joe coming through.

By now we didn't know who or what to believe, each doctor had his own opinion, nothing seemed to be coordinated.

It seemed this Monday was a day of "see what we can do for Joe." Dr. Yam called to ask my permission to do a bronchoscopy, which he said could be done by using the tube already in Joe's throat. They were looking for possible lung debris in the bronchial tubes. They told me afterwards they found no obstructions. The blood gases were averaging 64/67 taken every hour. Joe was put on the High Frequency Ventilator for a couple of hours, but blood gas levels were no better, so by 9 p.m. he was put back on PEEP.

We were told that same day that both lungs were now affected, so they had paralyzed Joe using the drug *pavulon* so he wouldn't move, the idea being to allow the respirator to do all the work and let Joe's lungs have more of a chance to heal.

From Physician Desk Reference (PDR), 33rd edition, 1979:

PAVULON
This drug should only be administered by adequately trained individuals familiar with its actions, characteristics and hazards.

ACTIONS: The most frequently reported observation is a slight rise in pulse rate.
Pavulon has no known effect on consciousness, the pain threshold, or cerebration.

WARNINGS: Pavulon should be administered in carefully adjusted dosages by or under the supervision of experienced clinicians, who are familiar with its actions and the possible complications that might occur following its use. The drug should not be administered unless facilities for INTUBATION, artificial respiration, oxygen therapy, and *reversal agents are immediately available.* The clinician must be prepared to assist or control respiration.

June 18—9:00 a.m. Dr. Ben D.O.:
Will increase PEEP to 18 cm H_20.
Attempt to High Frequency Ventilate.
Will de central line.
Slight dehydration shown—will increase fluids.

June 19—A spark of hope when I called the hospital at 9 a.m.! Joe's blood gases at 2 a.m. were 90 and at 9 a.m. they were 87, so the pressure of the respiratory machine was turned down to 80%. It seemed that the gases were the main concern and were at this point still being checked every hour. We were told that Joe would be given a lung scan this day.

During the 5–6 visiting hour, Carol and I went in to see Joe. It was quite disheartening to see him so completely paralyzed. We were told again his heart and kidneys are still in good shape. Oxygen level now set at 60 while blood gases were 62. His eye, face, and shoulders were still puffed up.

Dr. Yam told us he would be going on vacation in a couple of days and that a respiratory consultant from a nearby hospital would be looking after Joe in his absence.

They began feeding Joe through the stomach tube this day and he tolerated it well.

Wednesday, June 20 was Joe's 64th birthday. At 9:30 a.m. Dr. Yam answered the phone with an encouraging message: the oxygen level was 60-70, setting at 50. By 1 a.m. the gases had lowered, however, they had doubled the calorie intake. Debbie and I went to see Joe at 5 p.m. Most of the puffy swelling was down by now, his color was good, and since he had good bowel tones, they were giving him two types of feeding, one in his stomach (or intestine) through a needle, the other through the chest line. His heart was fine, blood gases about the same. How often we heard these same words!

I did feel that he looked comfortable and noted he was breathing at fourteen breaths per minute. "No happy birthday this year," Joe had written just a few days after surgery, and he was right.

I always tried to talk with the nurse in charge of Joe—if possible, they changed daily. This nurse expressed the opinion that he just needed time to heal.

Dr. Yam, the next day, Thursday the 21st of June, was very pleased with Joe's condition. His lungs were clear, most of the swelling was down, blood gases were up to 75 with oxygen pressure of 50 and there was talk of reducing it. All signs looked good. Dr. Yam also said it may take a week to reduce the oxygen and get Joe off the PEEP and onto the regular respirator. *A gradual weaning of medication to paralyze,* too, would be in order. Dr. Bow and Dr. Levy, another resident, are to be in attendance while Dr. Yam is on vacation. They kept changing assignments of substitutes.

Joe was no longer on morphine—he was back on valium—completely sedated and paralyzed. By 5 p.m. his blood gases were down to 64; air was still leaking out of the drain hose. The respiratory specialist from the other hospital, Dr. Gold, came to see Joe while I was there. He checked Joe's charts and said he couldn't think of anything more to do than Dr. Yam has already been doing. In his opinion, Joe still had a 50/50 chance.

On Friday, June 22, my 9:00 a.m. call to intensive care unit was answered by the nurse in charge who gave me all the latest information: the tube through the nose to stomach had been removed, Joe had three bowel movements, Dr. Hackett had removed all the staples but had left the silk stitches in and Joe's heart rate had increased once during the night to nearly 200. (I noted later in my study of this drug that the pavulon is noted for fast heart rate as one of its many side effects.)

> June 22—Some PAT 180/110 min c̄ response to verapamel Dr. Hackett, D.O.
>
> June 22, 1984—summary of results of portable lungs: There is a left lower lobe infiltrate felt to be consistent with pneumonia.

My call at 1 p.m. brought only the unsure answer that blood gases were down, all else okay, and that Dr. Hackett wanted to talk with me but would not be there at 5. The nurse said the problem is still ARDS.

I thought Dr. Hackett might have some good news, so I had Carol call him. He was very nice but told her things we already knew. He said he was still optimistic and we should hang in there.

At 4 p.m. Lew and I left to see Joe. Deb had a bad cold that she didn't want to take to him. We found him about the same except his position looked uncomfortable. I could tell his heart rate was somewhat increased, also noticed no air bubbles were coming from the drain tub. The specialist from the neighboring hospital was there, but he didn't talk with us this time.

> June 23, 1984—Chest tube became disconnected, 0900—chest tube leaking air.

Joe's nurse in the morning of June 23, when I called at 9:30 a.m. told me Dr. Hackett suggested backing off the sedation. She said she hadn't yet received any orders regarding this but told me, if they do back off, awakening would be gradual—it would take a while. I wondered as she talked how long a while, hours, days? She told me then that his heart rate was the same—all was the same.

When I called at 1:20 p.m. I was told Joe had received no sedation today but hadn't awakened yet. Dr. Hackett couldn't be reached. I wanted to hear from him just what his plan was in regard to the sedation. I was told he wanted to see what degree of alertness Joe might have, but I understood it should be down gradually and possibly with a reversal agent. I doubt Dr. Hackett knew this should be done. (I see nothing in the records about a reversal agent being administered.) At 5 p.m. when Carol, Kim, and I went in to see Joe, he was still completely sedated. We called the chaplain, thinking when Joe came around he'd want to see him. He assured us he'd check back again later to see if Joe had awakened.

June 24—at 9 a.m. the next day the nurse told me Joe had moved his mouth a little when she swabbed it out—also he coughed. His blood gases were still between 50 and 70 up and down.

Carol called Dr. Stone, another intern working with Joe, who said he was somewhat encouraged—he thinks the lung is healing but it will be a slow process.

The nurse at 1 p.m. said, "He is about the same." At 5 p.m. Deb and I couldn't wake him, but he was breathing on his own about six times a minute, was coughing some and hiccupping. His hands, arms, and legs were swollen, full of fluid and with the medication he was expelling lots of urine.

June 25—my call at 9 a.m. revealed that the respiratory doctor, Dr. Mat, made some changes in the ventilator yesterday; they were unsuccessful. Joe was still not awake; they said his chemistry may need altering. Dr. Gold and Dr. Mat were associates.

Carol and Kim came in at 5 p.m. to see Joe and to take me home. Joe opened his eyes for Carol and Kim. The chaplain came in and Joe opened his eyes for him, for me and again for Dr. Hackett. Both Dr. Key and Dr. Hackett seemed encouraged, particularly since Joe *was breathing on his own* (about 20 times a minute). Somehow Dr. Hackett grabbed any little change to make me think Joe was getting better, when I knew from the respiratory specialist that breathing on his own was not what he wanted him to do.

> June 26 —"PT condition unchanged—still depressed neurologically" Dr. Hackett, D.O.

On Tuesday, June 26th Joe was taken at 8:30 a.m. for a CAT scan, during which time he had his eyes open. I was so pleased when the nurse told me she had explained to him where he was, and following this she talked to him while she gave him a bath. We'd had a feeling Joe was being treated very impersonally because he couldn't talk. This didn't mean he couldn't think or couldn't hear. When the family talked to him, he responded with an occasional frown, a crooked smile, opened and closed his eyes and tried to move his head slightly. He knew us and knew we loved him, but he couldn't say a word.

That day, since Joe was more alert, I had gone to the hospital with Deb at 1 p.m., then waited in the ICU waiting room until I could see Joe again at 5 p.m. The respirator oxygen was now set at 65, the PEEP at 15, and blood gases were about the same.

The respiratory men from the nearby hospital normally made their rounds to see Joe at about this time. The Respiratory Doctor came in, checked Joe's lungs, then told us, "His left lung still has pneumonia." His manner said as much as "he doesn't have a chance." He said the next day he has planned to do a bronchoscopy, then he could get a sample of what was in the lung and better determine which antibiotic would be more effective. He very openly said, "He has had pneumonia all along!"

After talking with Dr. Mat who *didn't* say "he has a 50/50 chance, hang in there!" Debbie was quite upset. Each day we kept each other informed in detail; this time we called Carol and all three of us decided to go to talk with Dr. Small, our family doctor. It was about time we got some stories straight and some facts clear. We felt we were on some kind of a seesaw—up and down—or a merry-go-round—going around in circles. Dr. Small appeared to understand our dilemma and promised to work out something the next morning whereby we would converse with only one doctor—one who would make himself available each day to talk with us.

It was decided by the doctors to have Dr. Snow see one of us each day at 5 p.m. We thought this meant that Dr. Snow would correlate the treatments, plans and opinions of the doctors working with Joe's case, then would be able to intelligently report to us concerning Joe's progress. He promised to give us the truth—be it good or bad.

We soon found what we expected of Dr. Snow would not take place. On the first meeting of our new plan Dr. Snow told me he *didn't* feel that Joe had pneumonia; that he still had this ARDS, and that his left lung wasn't responding to treatment. He suggested reopening the incisions to look around for possible infection. He said he really felt Joe was strong enough to stand the surgery. The chaplain sat in on this conversation—also Dr. Key, an intern.

June 27—Joe's nurse said today Joe opened his eyes and squeezed her hand weakly. When Carol came in, we talked with Dr. Mat. He *still* contended Joe had pneumonia and had *very* little chance of survival.

He mentioned the bronchoscopy again, that he might do on Friday and as a last resort, give steroids. I told him of Dr. Snow's suggestion for further surgery, and it was his opinion that in no way could Joe stand this! Reverse opinions again! We were no better off in understanding what was happening. It seemed that mistakes were made, then covered up by another mistake—so it was just one vicious circle of events all happening to Joe who trusted these doctors *so* much.

> June 28—Summary Portable lungs: When review is made of previous examination there is felt to be some minimal improvement to the right upper lobe, otherwise the examination is smaller.

June 28—I could not go to the hospital this day as I planned because of severe stomach pains. So I called the ICU at 1 p.m. and found that the blood gases were about the same, too low. Dr. Mat had just seen Joe again and saw that he was breathing too much on his own, which was interfering with the respirator. So orders were given to sedate Joe again with *morphine.* I was also told Dr. Levy would be handling the case, a doctor I have yet even to see or meet.

By 5 p.m. my stomach pains had subsided, and Deb and Carol both joined me in talking with Dr. Hackett. I could not believe he had finally conferred with Dr. Mat and they now had the same opinion. He said Dr. Mat would be doing the bronchoscopy tomorrow (Friday), the purpose of which was to locate the infection, biopsy the mucus and/or fluid and better determine what antibiotic to use. Dr. Black, infection specialist, was now in on the case. Dr. Hackett also said the oxygen could become toxic after constant use and the lungs could become dry and hard. The nurse with Joe this day said she didn't know how Joe had held on this long.

> June 29—PT to have bronchoscopy.
> June 29—"Anorea was suspected." Dr. Nerr, D.O.

My friend of 30 years drove in from Ohio for a few days. It was so good to have her visit, particularly now. She gave me invaluable moral support. We had been in close contact about Joe, so we needed only to discuss recent developments to bring her up to date.

June 29th, our 43rd wedding anniversary, was, of course, a very unhappy anniversary! I don't think I mentioned it in talking to Joe—I remember thinking that he might get upset if he realized how long he had been here. Deb and Lew went to see him this a.m.. Debbie seemed to be quite successful at getting a response from Joe. Of course, questions had to be limited to what would get a "yes" or "no" answer. Joe would open his eyes when called, shake his head "no," frown if I moved the bed or if I'd touch his feet. Dr. Mat had me sign for the bronchoscopy, which was planned for 4:30 p.m. He spoke to us following this procedure and said he was surprised to find the right lung (upper lobe) still collapsed and containing a great amount of fluid which he suctioned out. In addition he said the left lung had some fluid (pneumonia) and he also asperated this. Dr. Mat said Joe tolerated the bronchoscopy very well. He was surprised to find Joe as alert as he was.

As my friend and I walked from the elevator we encountered the anesthetist, Dr. Fred. He seemed surprised to hear Joe wasn't doing well. I was, on the other hand, surprised to hear he was unaware of Joe's condition, for nearly everyone on the staff, admission clerks and nurses included, knew about Joe. Many of the nurses from the floor where Joe had been in March had been going into ICU to visit Joe periodically. Some of the nurses were asked not to visit him anymore in ICU. They were told they upset him. They felt bad about the turn of events since Joe had been so good prior to the surgery.

June 30—Joe was still responding to questions on June 30th., after a bit of prodding. His blood gases were 77 this morning and Dr. Key had removed the remaining stitches from the surgery. We both went to the hospital at 5 p.m. Joe was nonresponsive but finally did open his eyes, not focusing. I wonder what a great effort this must have been to try to respond, almost completely paralyzed and loaded with morphine. How much of his moments were conscious we'll never know, but to be trapped in a body that couldn't move, with a tube between the vocal cords so he couldn't even call out—must have been like being buried alive.

The tube into his throat had to be securely fastened with gauze srips so it wouldn't come out. However, since Joe couldn't speak up and say, "This is cutting me," I kept watch on it. At two different times I noticed the gauze so tight it brought blood. It really seems strange that in Intensive Care I had to point out a thing like this, which was so obvious.

Debbie had suggested that perhaps Joe should be getting some therapy. She was thinking of some moving of the limbs aside from and in addition to being turned periodically; from this some respiratory therapy was begun. The plan was to do percussion on the left side, then place Joe on his left side, head lowered, feet elevated, so as to have possible drainage. There were no good results from this; the idea was dismissed; the blood gases showed no improvement. I found that chest X-rays were scheduled for the next morning and an EEG Monday, July 2nd.

July 1984

July 1st—My friend was such a great help, cooking, trimming bushes, answering the phone, and today she offered to babysit our three-year-old grandson so that Debbie and I could get to the hospital by noon. Joe opened his eyes. That was all except for a small frown for Deb. His condition hadn't changed.

I talked with Dr. Black who said from the analysis of fluid taken by bronchoscopy, there really was not much infection. *They had stopped the antibiotics; the problem seemed to be mechanical.* Then I talked with Dr. Snow at 1:45 p.m. The current thought was that Joe has had an embolism (a blood clot in the brain stem, a stroke). Joe should not have been still paralyzed, the pavulon should have worn off in a couple of hours on Saturday, June 23rd. But Joe did not move a finger!

July 1— Condition stable.

Traveling to the hospital since January rather frequently, we had weathered many a storm, from sleet to hail to snow and ice, but never did it take so long for the trip home as one this Sunday. We had severe flooding on several routes and at one bridge we had to turn back and go ten miles out of our way. Water was well over the bridge. It took two hours to get home; it was normally a forty-five minute trip.

July 2nd—My friend, although off from her teaching job for the summer, had family obligations and left for her home in Pittsburgh. Her stay was all too short, but I was glad to have had her welcome help even for a few days and most especially for the moral support she gave me.

Debbie and Lew took Josh with us this July 2nd into ICU to see Joe. He smiled at Josh, opened his eyes when we called to him, also he nodded "yes" and "no" appropriately when Deb asked him questions.

Dr. Snow talked with us. He did not have a full report on the EEG or CAT scan taken earlier this day. He promised to call me the next day with these results. Evidently Joe's blood gases in early A.M. had been up to 90, so the machine (PEEP) was turned down to 55.

My friend, having arrived safely in Pittsburg, called me much concerned about Joe, encouraging us to get Joe out of that hospital and in to the doctor in Philadelphia. The girls worked on this last week and found a pulmonary specialist at a Philadelphia hospital who would accept the challenge of taking Joe as a patient. However, there was a problem of transporting Joe safely and they found most ambulances were not equipped to handle a respirator.

THIS DOCTOR TOLD CAROL HE WOULD MORE READILY ACCEPT JOE IF THERE WERE NO CANCER INVOLVED. HE THOUGHT THIS WOULD COMPLICATE THE ALREADY EXISTING PROBLEM, BUT HE WOULD TAKE CARE OF JOE IF WE COULD GET HIM THERE.

I waited all day for Dr. Snow's call, Tuesday, July 3rd, and finally I called *him.* He told me Joe's CAT Scan was okay (whatever that meant) and that the EEG showed some diffusion. He said the neurologist thought there had been a thrombosis at the brain stem.

July—"An intersectial and alveolar disease noted in left lower lung zone."

July 3—"Renal failure" 10 A.M.

July 3— Problem list by Dr. Hackett—
Nine are listed:
#2. Respiratory failure ARDS
versus lung injury 2° RT.

This is the first mention of lung injury except what we had heard from the intern about the actual surgery. I wonder is this an admission that the lung was injured?

Debbie, having had several years experience with geriatrics, was good at getting Joe's attention. She yelled at him close to his ear until she got some response. She was sure the nurses weren't offering any stimulus, assuming Joe couldn't hear—just because he couldn't talk or move.

Joe was again responsive to Debbie's questions and to Lew's. Dr. Snow witnessed him answering Lew. His blood gases ran about the same. In talking with Dr. Snow, he had a couple of points to discuss with me. He asked if we would want Joe to live paralyzed. Apparently he had conceded that Joe's paralysis would not reverse itself. He also brought up the topic of money, and, in particular, Joe's hospital bill. He said we would not get a bill from the hospital nor from the surgeons. This was because they agreed to accept whatever Medicare and "65 Special" pay. I realized some time later that Dr. Snow was telling me about the financial situation in hopes that we would *not* move Joe to another hospital. He tried to explain that he was on a hospital committee and as of July 1st this was a new arrangement. I didn't believe him, but knew I'd find out later.

July 4th—Carol, Kim, and Kelley came to get me at noon to go see Joe. He looked very uncomfortable, the way he was positioned. His nurse today said he had been weighed at 250 pounds (which probably included about 25 pounds of fluid). He had a mild temperature of 99.6°, and I noticed he was sweating. He smiled at Carol and Kim and it seemed as though he focused on me as I tried to get his attention. We could never be sure how much he could hear or whether he worried about his condition, whether he wanted to ask us questions, whether he thought he was going to die. The predicament could be compared to being buried alive—being trapped in a body that couldn't move nor could he speak.

When I called Thursday, July 5th, between 9 and 10 a.m., the nurse informed me his blood gases were 80 which sounded like good news, but he had a low-grade temperature. At 1 p.m when I went in, Joe was getting more blood. There were two pints ordered; I believe #9 and #10. His red blood cells (carrying oxygen) were low, white blood cell count was a little elevated.

Both the girls and I at this point were all in favor of moving Joe to another hospital. We each had a part in making some plans to move him on Saturday, July 7th.

July 5— "0900 PT remains unresponsive"
Dr. Hackett

July 5— Scan of chest—Summary—the examimation is felt to be consistent with radiation fibrotis disease.

Eight p.m., July 5th, Dr. Gold (the respiratory doctor) called, telling me Joe's right lung had improved some since he had done the bronchoscopy. His left lung still had fluid. He said he had seen patients as sick get well; his condition could reverse, his kidneys were stable, his heart good—in his opinion he *could* be moved.

Here it was again, opposite opinions—false hope—were any of these doctors telling the truth? Could we believe any of them? Could we trust any of them? It seemed they were all "cut from the same pattern." Dr. Gold had come on this case with very negative feelings from the beginning—now after the others were conceding there was not much hope for Joe—Dr. Gold says he could recover.

I cannot imagine a group of professionals acting more *unprofessional* than these doctors have! Each gave his own opinion regardless of that of his associate or colleague. Nothing seemed to be coordinated. It seemed that orders were given for tests or treatment on impulse to make it look like something was being done for Joe.

> July 6— "Lab at hospital not notified of positive cultures from branch washings taken 6/29 and sent to AML in an attempt to establish diagnosis."
> "*AML failed to notify lab at hospital. Upon receipt of positive cultures, erythromycin restarted.*"
>
> Recommends: Watch for other super infections. Previous broncho studies for legionelle were negative. Cannot be sure though and doubt epidemiology will be helpful.
>
> Dr. Black, Infection Specialist

When Carol called the hospital July 6th at 10 a.m., she was told there was some infection in the bloodstream, they didn't know the source. I couldn't imagine why Dr. Black, the infection specialist, had taken Joe off antibiotics last week. Carol was also told that Joe was getting some physical therapy (which we had requested a week ago), also that they would be taking Joe's chest tube out and in addition planned to do a tracheotomy that day.

Although I wanted that tube out of Joe's throat as much as he did, I didn't want any more botched up surgery in this hospital. I asked

Dr. Snow hold off on the tracheotomy and call me before he did anything.

Friday, July 6th—Dr. Snow promised to call me before he did the tracheotomy and he kept his word. I had (with the help of Carol and Deb) spent nearly all of Thursday, July 5th, making plans to move Joe from this hospital. Having succeeded with these plans, I knew when Dr. Snow called I would tell him what I intended to do.

"We are going to move Joe to another hospital and I would like your cooperation," I began, knowing we would need help to move him safely.

Dr. Snow said, "The main trouble you'll have is to find a doctor who will take him."

My quick answer was, "We have already found someone. We will need a respiratory therapist and a registered nurse to go along."

Dr. Snow's voice had an element of surprise as he asked, "Will you be up today?"

I answered, "Yes, we'll be there at 5 p.m."

"I'll see you then," he very quickly answered, and, without saying "Goodbye," he hung up.

Carol, Deb, Lew and Josh and myself met Dr. Snow and Dr. Small in the ICU waiting room around 5:15 p.m. after we had visited Joe. (Dr. Small was off duty but was called in by Dr. Snow as a witness to what we were going to talk about.) Joe was, as I suspected, comatose, Dr. Snow confirmed this when I asked. Dr. Snow began by asking the question, "Do you remember we told you sometime ago we had sent five slides out?"

I had never heard mention of five slides, so I'm sure I looked very puzzled. (Dr. Snow had done this to me before, I believe it was a habit of his, trying to make others believe he had previously told them something.)

I immediately said, "I don't remember hearing anything about five slides."

Dr. Snow then explained, "Five slides of the biopsy were sent to five different pathologists, and just *this very day* (Friday) the fifth one had been returned, negative, no cancer."

My reaction was that I had been previously told that the cells around the area in question were benign and that the cells biopsied from the stomach and esophagus stumps were also benign.

So I said, "Yes, this is what I'd been told."

Dr. Snow then said, "I don't believe you understand what I'm telling you. These five slides were of the *original biopsy taken before surgery.*"

I couldn't believe what I was hearing! I asked, "You mean to tell me that Joe had *no* cancer from the beginning?"

He said this was true and went on to explain. The pathologist from this hospital, Dr. Norton, had been on vacation, when a pathologist from Philadelphia (Dr. Falco, his name given readily when we asked) had taken his place and had read the slides wrong!! There *never had been any cancer, never had been any tumor! Just a BIG MISTAKE!* There was a moment of dead silence. It seemed like some kind of a movie script, certainly not something that could have happened to me. I could find no words to express all the emotions I felt at this time.

After what seemed a long time, Dr. Small spoke up and said, "We're really sorry, this is the first this has ever happened in this hospital."

So many things went through my head this moment; how could I keep my composure and at the same time express my feelings? So this was why all had been such a turmoil; why so many opposite opinions; this was why the silent treatment we kept getting from the nurses; this was why we were discouraged about moving Joe from this hospital to another.

Finally I forced myself to ask, "Who knows or has known about this?"

Dr. Snow answered, "I suppose nearly all the doctors involved."

I said, "You can rest assured there will be a lot more people know about this before it's all over—the Reader's Digest should be a good place to begin telling what happened here."

Such a mild threat in comparison to what I really would like to have said! I felt so completely helpless, what could any of us do to help now?

I can remember commenting about the fact the esophagus wasn't biopsied again following radiation and before surgery. I was told, "This is procedure."

My answer was, "I know it's *your* procedure, but your procedure needs to be changed! The patient at this point should not be pressured into immediate surgery and each thing should be *double checked* before a patient is subjected to such a life-threatening ordeal." Both doctors sat staring at me, I couldn't understand that they acted like none of this was their doing, like it wasn't their fault.

We left the hospital shortly, Debbie and Lew going to their car, and I was going to ride with Carol. As Carol and I approached the sidewalk, Dr. Small was just getting into his car and pulled up to speak to us. He was very apologetic. Dr. Hackett, who had been in the hospital during our shocking news, then came out the front door, and, seeing Carol and me still there, had the look of "Gosh, I came out too soon, I'm caught!" There was nothing he could do but come over to us, hanging his head, stumbling words of guilty sorrow.

Saturday, July 7th—Before we could begin our plans for moving Joe, Dr. Gold called from the hospital early in the morning. He said Joe had made a turn for the worse and perhaps the family would want to come up.

Deb and Lew left immediately since they had planned to go to the hospital early and were already dressed. Carol, Kim and Tom picked me up and we all went to the hospital.

> July 7—Eight a.m., 12:30, 2:30, D.O.M. Mike Family N and present attending—Gaynor, Hackett, Gold, Ray, Ryen. Signed Ryen
>
> July 7 — Portable lung X-ray
> The interstifial and alveolar (Air cells, lungs) findings in lungs are unchanged when compared with prior films. Heart is *not* abnormal, Endotracheal tube is in satisfactory position. Concidental finding concerns a moderate amount of gas seen in bowels below the diaphragm. WEB/bam (typed)

Joe was unresponsive and two nurses worked continuously injecting bicarb with a large syringe into the IV shunt, antibiotics, etc. He was in a coma, his kidneys failing and blood pressure very low; edema all over his body. He was getting 100% oxygen from the PEEP machine, yet his blood gases showed only 30% oxygen. They were all working like crazy, yes, *crazy!* They couldn't save him now!

"Procedure" seemed to supercede common sense. This thing called "Code Blue" might be fine in an emergency, but when a patient has been dying for several days, why not let him die in peace?"

Thirty-three days of covering mistakes, guessing, each doctor doing his own thing and now, when the inevitable is happening, the staff goes crazy putting on an act "to save his life."

JULY 7th—ON THIS DAY JOE HAD HIS TWENTY-NINTH CHEST X-RAY MADE IN THIRTY-ONE DAYS PLUS FOUR OTHERS OF THE ESOPHAGUS, PHARYNX AND CAT SCANS.

The billing shows *four chest X-rays* made in this one day, yet we, the family, saw none being made (we were there from early morning).

Dr. Hackett came in the room, motioned for me to come out to talk. We stood face to face in the doorway and he said, "We're doing all we can for Joe."

My reply was, "You've not done one *good* thing for Joe since he came here!"

He answered, "You're absolutely right!" and walked off. This was the last I ever saw of this surgeon; never an "I'm sorry," a card or a condolence.

All of us stayed all day, going in and out of Joe's room. It was too late to move him to the Philadelphia hospital. The hospital chaplain was on this day finally a help to us, this being part of his job. However, being on the hospital's payroll, I had begun to mistrust him like the rest. When had he heard of the mistake by the pathologist? Was he, too, trying to cover up for the mistakes made by others on the staff? He spent nearly all the rest of the day trying to convince me he was on our side; especially since I told him I thought all of them were "cut from the same pattern."

By 4:45 p.m. the nurse suggested we leave the room while they turned Joe. While turning him, they lost him. He died with that dreaded tube still between his vocal cords, never had a chance to talk to any of us since before the surgery, thirty-three days before. The chaplain came out to tell us everyone was in Joe's room working on him to revive him. Then he came out about 5 p.m. with the word Joe was gone. He and an intern expressed their sympathy. We never heard a thing from any of the doctors except from Dr. Small, our family doctor, who did seem concerned.

Perhaps if I had been stronger in my plea for Joe to have another opinion aside from this hospital or another surgeon at another hospital—he might have conceded and would now be alive. Joe was strong-willed; I'm not sure he would ever have changed his mind without some real basis. He wanted to be here till year 2,000 and to see his only grandson, Josh, graduate. He kept telling everyone he felt like a million bucks and repeating his positive attitude quotations over and over. He had planned much for our future together.

I have lost my partner, my companion, my love, my lifeline. I now find myself single in a couple's society, branded by the name "widow" after forty-three years of marriage. I don't know how I'll cope with this.

Will this matter to those responsible for the death of my husband? Should doctors be allowed to continue inadequate acts, to continue to play GOD with a patient's life, covering up for each other after blunders and deceptions?

Joe was a very young and healthy sixty-four. He had no diabetes, had a good strong heart, good muscle tone, no breathing problems—could easily have lived another twenty years. His father lived till he was eighty-five, his grandmother till ninety-three, his grandfather till eighty-six. Joe was killed in the hospital at sixty-four!

EPILOGUE

Conflict Of Opinions

At one point, near the end, Dr. Hackett and Dr. Snow were considering further surgery, of going back into the same incisions to look for infection. They thought Joe could stand the surgery.

I asked Dr. Gold and Dr. Mat, (respiratory doctors on the case) about this the next day . They said, "No way can he stand more surgery!"

In fact, on five major issues at this point, the surgeons' opinions were in direct opposition to the respiratory doctors' opinions:

1. Surgeons said, "Operate again."
   Respiratory doctors said, "No way!"
2. Surgeons said his lungs were clear.
   Respiratory doctors said he has pneumonia.
3. Surgeons said it's good he's breathing on his own.
   Respiratory doctors do not want him to interfere with respirator.
4. Surgeons said blood gases aren't all that important.
   Respiratory doctors said the blood gases are the important factor.
5. Surgeons said take Joe off sedatives.
   Respiratory doctors said put Joe back on sedatives.

These greatly opposite opinions were expressed in the *same two days* and finally, on the third day, the doctors got together and agreed on all five points with the opinions of the respiratory doctors.

In Retrospect

Looking back, it seems rather ironic that so many things contributed to Joe's death, yet if any *one* contributing factor had been nonexistent, this story could have had an entirely different ending.

Contributing factors to Joe's death were the following:

1. The Pathologist who erroneously read the biopsy to be malignant.
2. The Radiologist who did radiation treatments on "hearsay."
3. The Infections Specialist who didn't follow up with the lab on results of the bronch washings and left Joe without the antibiotics for a week.
4. The Respiratory doctor who left Joe after rendering him paralyzed, took off on a two-week vacation and didn't return until after Joe died.
5. The Chaplain, who works closely with PR—who induced Joe to return to that hospital promising he'd be there for him, but was nowhere to be found for a week after surgery when Joe needed him. We still wonder just when *he* heard the news that Joe had unnecessary surgery.
6. The respiratory specialist who kept changing his opinion from completely negative to positive about Joe's condition. What pressure was he under?
7. The surgeon who continuously painted the picture rosy when all the while his associate was reporting, "He's deteriorating."
8. The chief surgeon, last but most contributing, who, because of "procedure," operated even after he saw no reason for it, lacerated and removed the spleen, bruised the right lung, cut the lung, knew immediately there was no cancer and kept it from the family. His ego and reputation being more important than the life of his patient (my husband), was not man enough to admit to Joe or to me that he didn't want to do this surgery, did do these things enumerated—thus contributing to Joe's death. (Substantiated in Coroner's Report; see page 61).

If any *one* of these men could have done differently, Joe might have been saved. And if any of these had dared to let me know the truth from the beginning and had spent their time trying to save Joe instead of trying so hard to cover up—Joe might have lived.

Final Pathological Diagnosis

Coroner's Report

One of the chaplain's duties at this hospital was to solicit bodily organs for donations. Joe had mentioned, while he was home, that he and the chaplain had discussed this topic and at one point Joe had said, "Well, he got what he wanted." This, we took to mean that, yes, Joe had donated some parts of his body. However, upon questioning, this was denied by the chaplain. This could have been a problem.

Since we were so unsure of the reason for Joe' death and also, due to the fact we no longer had trust or faith in anyone from this particular hospital, in requesting a post-mortem examination, we specifically requested that the autopsy be done by a pathologist *not* connected with this hospital.

Another mistake on our part! We accepted the chaplain's advice in using the County Coroner (pro tem) whose office was only a few blocks from the hospital. Although this pathologist was aware of our request, he permitted the hospital's pathologist to observe the performance of this autopsy and gave him tissue samples for his own histological examination. We were no further ahead than if we had engaged the hospital's pathologist.

Diagnosis as this coroner reported it:

The cause of death: Bronchopneumonia
The manner of death: Natural

In his description, the lungs revealed reddish cut surfaces and the coroner stated that conditions found in the area of the diaphragm had apparently been used as part of the operative procedure in a way very difficult to describe. He also found *no* lesions.

Questions Unanswered

1. If I hadn't told of moving Joe to another hospital, would we ever have known that Joe went through eighteen radiation treatments, sixty-seven days in the hospital, major surgery, tolerated a tube in his throat, was paralyzed and died all because one pathologist made a mistake?

2. Do these surgeons think for one minute that their hands are clean? Joe could have lived after surgery whether or not he had cancer.

3. What mistakes did the SURGEONS MAKE? Why was number one on the diagnosis list "lacerated spleen"?

4. Why did the doctors keep avoiding us most of the time, and most of the nurses, too, in ICU, who didn't want to talk to us? We had to go after the nurses nearly every day to find out anything about Joe's day. He couldn't tell us anything with a breathing tube between his vocal cords. He was trapped in a body completely paralyzed. He couldn't move a finger.

5. Why did the respiratory doctor in charge leave on an extended vacation just having rendered Joe paralyzed with a very potent drug—pavulon?

6. The surgeon who took him off this drug, did he do this properly? Joe never did become *un*paralyzed.

7. What was the radiologist radiating? How and on what did he center the radiation? He acted on hearsay, he didn't have Joe's records when he began, didn't see any X-rays or *recent* tests results.

8. Why was the surgeon in charge so long after surgery?

9. Did the other doctors refuse to become a part of this after the respiratory doctor left on vacation? We were told three other doctors would be in charge of Joe's case while this doctor was on vacation. Strange, we never saw any of them. Did they refuse to participate?

10. What part did our family doctor play in this? When did he know that Joe was operated on for nothing? I would like to trust him,

but I think he, too, is "cut from the same pattern" as the other doctors.

11. In March, when Joe was first diagnosed, I talked with the doctor who looked at the problem with the endoscope, (3/9/84). I asked him the size of the tumor he said he saw in Joe's esophagus. He answered rather curtly, "I don't know; I didn't measure it!" He kept telling Joe he was so optimistic about the surgeons being able to get 100% of the tumor and that the surgery would effect a complete cure; promising anything to make sure Joe would have the surgery. Could he have known there was no tumor, no malignancy? He looked down twice with the endoscope and even after the second time he said, "The tumor is still present." How could he be so positive and yet so wrong? Is he any more without fault than the pathologist who made the first mistake?

12. Why on earth did the infection specialist stop the antibiotics a few days before Joe died? Anyone could tell that he had infection, his temperature rose immediately. From then on it was all downhill absolutely. This doctor didn't bother to check on the lab report until a *week* after the bronchoscopy.

13. Was there a conspiracy to confuse the family or were the many conflicts due to covering up from the first mistake? They must have really hated to tell our family the truth after keeping the secret from us for thirty days.